HEROES OF BLACK HISTORY

BOOKER T. WASHINGTON

BY JANEY LEVY

Gareth Stevens
PUBLISHING

Please visit our website, www.garethstevens.com. For a free color catalog of all our high-quality books, call toll free 1-800-542-2595 or fax 1-877-542-2596.

Library of Congress Cataloging-in-Publication Data
Names: Levy, Janey, author.
Title: Booker T. Washington / Janey Levy.
Description: New York : Gareth Stevens Publishing, [2021] | Series: Heroes of Black history | Includes bibliographical references and index. | Contents: Meet Booker T. Washington – A Hard Start in Life – A Thirst for Learning – Tuskegee – The "Atlanta Compromise" – Advisor to Presidents – A Complicated Legacy.
Identifiers: LCCN 2019043999 | ISBN 9781538258088 (library binding) | ISBN 9781538258064 (paperback) | ISBN 9781538258071 (6 Pack) | ISBN 9781538258095 (ebook)
Subjects: LCSH: Washington, Booker T., 1856-1915--Juvenile literature. | African Americans--Biography--Juvenile literature. | Educators--United States--Biography--Juvenile literature.
Classification: LCC E185.97.W4 L48 2021 | DDC 370.92 [B]--dc23
LC record available at https://lccn.loc.gov/2019043999

First Edition

Published in 2021 by
Gareth Stevens Publishing
111 East 14th Street, Suite 349
New York, NY 10003

Designer: Laura Bowen
Editor: Monika Davies

Photo credits: Cover, p. 1 (Booker T. Washington) Interim Archives/Contributor/Archive Photos/Getty Images; cover, pp. 1–32 (background image), 6, 7 (interior), 9, 13 (both), 15 (house), 19 (campus), 21 (both) courtesy of the Library of Congress; p. 5 Everett Historical/Shutterstock.com; p. 7 Jeff Greenberg/Contributor/Universal Images Group Editorial/Getty Images; p. 11 Douglas W. Reynolds/Wikimedia Commons; p. 15 (map) JUN KAWAGUCHI/Shutterstock.com; p. 15 (woods) Jon Marc Lyttle/Shutterstock.com; p. 17 SaveRivers/Wikimedia Commons; p. 19 (students) Photo 12/Contributor/Universal Images Group Editorial/Getty Images; p. 23 C. M. Battey/Stringer/Hulton Archive/Getty Images; p. 25 Buyenlarge/Contributor/Archive Photos/Getty Images; p. 26 Hulton Archive/ Stringer/Archive Photos/Getty Images; p. 27 Robert Abbott Sengstacke/Contributor/Archive Photos/ Getty Images.

Printed in the United States of America

Some of the images in this book illustrate individuals who are models. The depictions do not imply actual situations or events.

CPSIA compliance information: Batch #CS20GS: For further information contact Gareth Stevens, New York, New York at 1-800-542-2595.

CONTENTS

Words in the glossary appear in **bold** type the first time they are used in the text.

MEET BOOKER T. WASHINGTON

Some have called Booker T. Washington the most famous black man in the United States from 1895 to 1915. Born into slavery, he managed to get an education through hard work. He later went on to become a champion for education for black people. When the **American Civil War** led to the end of slavery, Booker believed education offered black people the best way to get ahead in their lives.

Even with all of Booker's fame and **influence**, not everyone supported his approach to improving black people's position in society. Inside this book, you'll learn about the life of this important educator and leader.

JIM CROW

Booker's fame was at its height during the time of Jim Crow laws in the South. These laws, named after an offensive term for a black man, limited black people's rights and freedoms. They limited black people's voting rights and forced black people and white people to use separate parks, drinking fountains, and more.

Many also name Booker as one of the most significant black educators of the late 1800s and early 1900s.

A HARD START IN LIFE

On April 5, 1856, a black woman named Jane gave birth to a son in Franklin County, Virginia. She named him Booker Taliaferro. Jane was a slave, so her son was a slave too. The baby's father was an unknown white man. Booker T. Washington had just been born, and already life was hard. It soon became harder. The American Civil War erupted when Booker was just 5 years old.

After the war ended in 1865, all slaves were emancipated, or freed from the control or power of an owner. But this didn't mean life suddenly became untroubled for freed slaves.

THE CIVIL WAR (1861–1865)

Northern states (the Union) and Southern states (the Confederacy) fought the Civil War over slavery. The North had a more **industrial** economy. The South had a farming economy that depended on labor from slaves. Southerners feared President Abraham Lincoln would end slavery. So, Southern states seceded from, or left, the United States and formed the Confederacy.

ABRAHAM LINCOLN, 1863

Booker grew up on a plantation, or a large farm. This is a reconstructed, or rebuilt, kitchen cabin that's similar to the one Booker and his mother lived in for the first 9 years of his life.

In 1865, after spending the first 9 years of his life as a slave, the newly free Booker went with his mother to Malden, West Virginia, to join his stepfather. There, he worked with his stepfather at a salt furnace. It was hard labor. They shoveled salt crystals into barrels and packed them down until the barrels reached the correct weight. Then, after all his hard work, his stepfather kept his pay.

Booker left the salt furnace behind to work in a coal mine when he was 10. It was also unpleasant work, but there was a bright spot: He attended school for a while.

PARADISE

Booker wrote in his autobiography, *Up from Slavery,* about the glimpses he had into schoolhouses as a young slave: "I had the feeling that to get into a schoolhouse and study in this way would be about the same as getting into paradise."

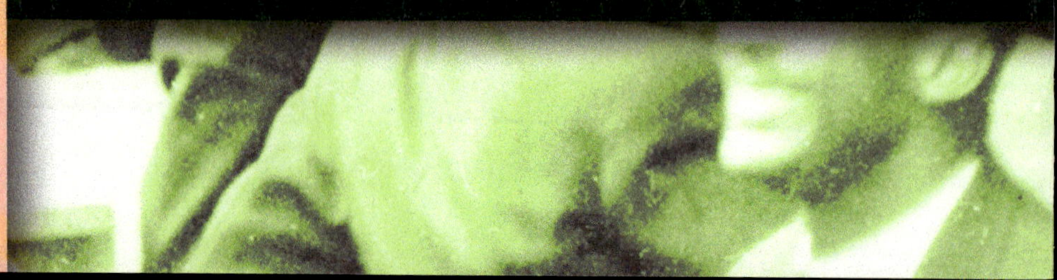

In 1865, a 9-year-old Booker became a member of the African Zion Baptist Church.

A THIRST FOR LEARNING

Booker was set on getting an education. In 1872, when he was 16, he left Malden, first hopping on a train and then walking the final miles to the Hampton Normal and Agricultural Institute in Hampton, Virginia. He had no money, so he worked at the school as a janitor to pay for his food and a place to sleep. The head of the school arranged for a wealthy person to pay for Booker's classes.

In 1875, the young man who was born a slave, then forced to work in a salt furnace and coal mine, graduated with honors. He was even chosen to speak at his graduation service.

WHAT'S IN A NAME?

As a former slave, Booker didn't have a last name. He was always known simply as "Booker." But when he started going to school, other children had two names, and he felt he should too. Booker chose his stepfather's first name, Washington, to be his last name and became Booker T. (for Taliaferro) Washington.

A "normal school" is a school for training teachers. Today, Hampton Normal and Agricultural Institute is Hampton University. This is how Hampton looks today.

Booker believed strongly in the value of education, not just for himself, but for all black people. Following his graduation from Hampton, Booker headed back to Malden to teach. He taught black children during the day and black adults at night.

After two years of teaching, Booker went back to school at Wayland Seminary in Washington, DC. Unlike the courses at Hampton, which covered farming skills and proper manners in addition to **academic** subjects, the courses at Wayland were all academic. Booker believed the practical education Hampton offered was superior. In 1879, he went back to Hampton as a teacher.

AN EDUCATIONAL PHILOSOPHY

During his years at Hampton, Booker formed strong ideas about the best education for black people in the United States. His ideas were greatly affected by the head of the school, Samuel Chapman Armstrong. Booker felt the best kind of education would give great attention to practical skills and ways black students could improve their lives.

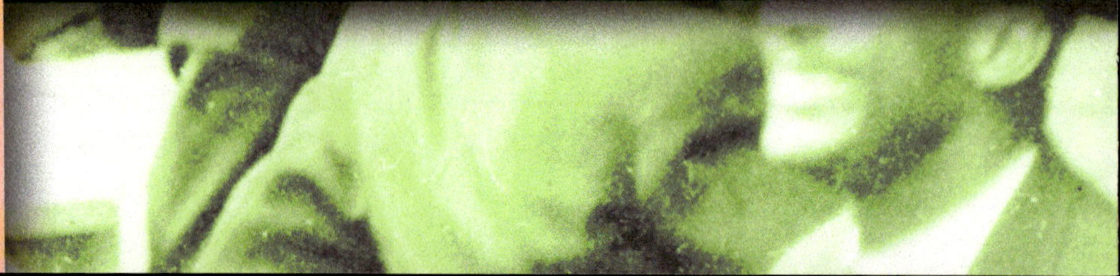

GEOGRAPHY CLASS AT HAMPTON, 1899

BRICKLAYING CLASS AT HAMPTON, 1899

Booker believed that an education should connect classroom learning with day-to-day life experiences.

TUSKEGEE

In 1881, Armstrong had a proposal for Booker. Armstrong had received a letter from some men in Alabama. They wanted him to suggest a principal for a new school to be built in Tuskegee. The school would be a teacher-training school for black people. The letter asked Armstrong to advise of a white person who could lead the school, but he wanted to give them Booker's name. Booker agreed to Armstrong's proposal, and the men in Alabama accepted his application.

But when Booker arrived in Tuskegee, he didn't find a school. There was no land or buildings, nor any money to buy them. There was only money to pay teachers.

THE ORIGIN OF THE TUSKEGEE SCHOOL

Lewis Adams, a freed slave, and George W. Campbell, a white man who once owned slaves, came up with the idea for the Tuskegee school. In 1880, the Alabama State **Legislature** passed a bill approving money for a teacher-training school for black people. Alabama's governor signed the bill on February 12, 1881.

IMPORTANT PLACES IN BOOKER'S LIFE

The places shown in red on this map were important in Booker's life and education.

Many people would likely feel discouraged, or without hope, about the situation Booker encountered. But Booker didn't let it get him down. He set about to make the school happen. His first goal was to get the two things he knew he needed to start: students and the support of local white people.

The school opened on July 4, 1881. The first classes were in a small shanty, or hut. The school didn't even own the shanty! A local black church had loaned the shanty to the school. It was a small beginning, but it was still a beginning. Plans were already underway for something much bigger.

ALABAMA'S BLACK POPULATION

When Alabama became a state in 1819, there were more than 38,000 black people living as slaves in the state. More than 435,000 black people were living as slaves in Alabama when the American Civil War started. When Booker arrived to set up the Tuskegee school, Alabama's black population was over 600,000.

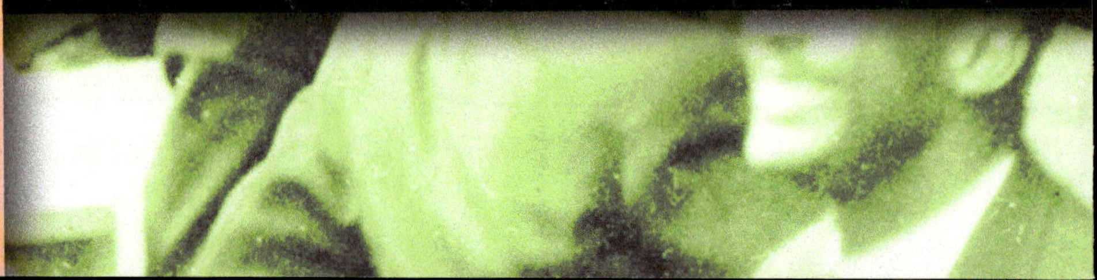

This is the church that loaned the shanty that first housed the Tuskegee school. The building shown here is a modern one. The building that was there in Booker's time no longer exists.

BREAKING AWAY

Booker borrowed money from a friend at Hampton and used it to buy an abandoned 100-acre (40 ha) plantation on the edge of Tuskegee. The students then built the school themselves! They first built a kiln, or furnace, to create bricks. The bricks were then used to build the school's buildings. Soon, the students had built a classroom, dining hall, chapel, and a building for girls to live in.

Just seven years after the school opened on 100 acres (40 ha) of land, it had expanded to 540 acres (220 ha). The school was known as the Tuskegee Normal and Industrial Institute, and it had more than 400 students.

TUSKEGEE AT 25

By the time Tuskegee Institute was 25 years old, the school was made of 83 buildings and had grown to cover around 2,000 acres (810 ha). The total value of the land, buildings, and school equipment was almost $832,000. More than 1,500 students attended the school. Classes offered training in 37 different fields.

TUSKEGEE CAMPUS, 1916

HISTORY CLASS AT TUSKEGEE INSTITUTE, 1906

True to Booker's educational beliefs, students learned practical skills such as carpentry, cabinet-making, shoemaking, farming, and cooking.

THE "ATLANTA COMPROMISE"

By 1895, Booker was such a towering black leader that he was invited to speak at the Cotton States and International **Exposition** held in Atlanta, Georgia. He gave a speech in which he explained his ideas about the best ways for black people to advance and acquire **equality** in society.

Booker didn't believe black people should demand immediate social and political equality. He argued black people should first learn practical skills—such as those taught at Tuskegee—so they could show they could earn their own way and contribute to society. He believed equality would naturally follow.

ACCEPTING SEGREGATION

Segregation, or the forced separation of races or classes, was a **reality** of the time, and Booker urged black people to accept it in these words from his speech: "In all things that are purely social we can be separate as the fingers, yet one as the hand in all things essential [necessary] to mutual [shared] progress."

BOOKER T. WASHINGTON, 1895

THE COTTON STATES AND INTERNATIONAL EXPOSITION ATLANTA, GEORGIA, 1895

Booker was only 39 years old when he was invited to speak in Atlanta in 1895.

Many white people were comfortable with Booker's approach. Some black people also agreed with Booker's approach. But others disagreed. Black leaders such as W.E.B. Du Bois and William Monroe Trotter were speaking out about the lack of equality between black people and white people. They thought more needed to be done to challenge the **discrimination** black people faced.

Du Bois was especially unhappy about the ideas in Booker's speech. He called the speech the "Atlanta Compromise," and he meant this name in a negative, or bad, way. In a compromise, each side gives up something to reach an agreement. But Du Bois felt Booker was giving up too much.

W.E.B. DU BOIS (1868–1963)

Du Bois was a highly educated university professor. At one point, he was friends with Booker. Du Bois once believed studying people would help solve **inequality** issues between black people and white people. But the terrible realities of continuing discrimination led him to decide only active protest would bring about change.

W.E.B. Du Bois was one of the founders of the National Association for the Advancement of Colored People (NAACP), though he later left the NAACP.

ADVISOR TO PRESIDENTS

In the early 1900s, the man who began life as a slave became an advisor to presidents. In 1901, President Theodore Roosevelt sent an invitation to Booker asking him to have dinner at the White House. No black leader had been asked to dine at the White House before.

So, how exactly did Booker advise President Roosevelt? At the time, there were certain government jobs that were commonly given to black people. Booker gave suggestions as to who could fill those positions. Roosevelt wasn't the only president to seek Booker's advice. When William Howard Taft became president after Roosevelt, Booker also advised Taft in the same way.

A BUSY TIME FOR BOOKER

Booker visited the White House during a busy time in his life. He remained head of the Tuskegee Normal and Industrial Institute. In 1900, he founded the National Negro Business League to support businesses run by black people. In 1901, he published the story of his life, *Up from Slavery*.

Booker's visit to the White House angered both white people and black people. Many white people thought a black person shouldn't visit the White House. Some black people thought Booker was being too agreeable to white people.

Booker didn't just have influence with American presidents. He was also friends with wealthy, powerful white businessmen such as Andrew Carnegie and John D. Rockefeller. Booker asked these men to provide funding and support for different types of schools in the South for black people.

As an advisor to presidents and friend of wealthy businessmen, Booker exercised great power during this period. But Woodrow Wilson, who became president in 1913, didn't want Booker's advice. Booker's influence lessened. At the same time, the views and voices of people like Du Bois gained strength. Booker died in 1915 as the world was changing.

THE END

Booker became ill while he was in New York City in late 1915. He spent a week in a hospital there, then returned to Tuskegee. He died there on November 14. His funeral was held in the Tuskegee Institute chapel on November 17. Almost 8,000 people came to his funeral to honor him.

25TH ANNIVERSARY OF TUSKEGEE INSTITUTE CELEBRATION, 1906

Booker was determined to be home when he died. He said, "I was born in the South, have lived all my life in the South, and expect to die and be buried in the South."

A COMPLICATED LEGACY

Booker T. Washington was a **complicated** man who left a complicated **legacy**. From his beginnings in slavery, he acquired an education and then built a great educational institute for black people at a time when few others existed. He advised presidents and was friends with powerful white business leaders.

However, he also urged black people to accept segregation and not immediately demand equal rights. He wanted black people to take a quiet path to equality. He didn't speak out against acts of violence against black people. The path he chose brought him great power and honor, but also great blame by some.

A SECRET SIDE TO BOOKER

Publicly, Booker urged black people to take the quiet path to equality. But he was much more active in secret than people realized. He financed and encouraged court cases that protested segregation and efforts to keep black people from voting. It was another side to this complicated man.

THE LIFE OF BOOKER T. WASHINGTON

APRIL 5, 1856	Booker is born in Franklin County, Virginia.
1865	Booker is freed from slavery, moves to Malden, West Virginia, and starts working at a salt furnace.
1866	Booker starts working in coal mine, attends school occasionally, and takes "Washington" as his last name.
1872	Booker starts school at Hampton Normal and Agricultural Institute in Hampton, Virginia.
1875	Booker graduates from Hampton and returns to Malden to teach.
1879	Booker returns to Hampton to teach.
1881	Booker arrives in Tuskegee and begins to build the Tuskegee Institute.
1895	Booker gives his "Atlanta Compromise" speech.
1900	Booker founds the National Negro Business League.
1901	Booker publishes *Up from Slavery* and becomes advisor to President Theodore Roosevelt.
NOVEMBER 14, 1915	Booker dies.

GLOSSARY

academic: having to do with schools and education, but not practical skills

American Civil War: a war fought from 1861 to 1865 in the United States between the Union (the Northern states) and the Confederacy (the Southern states)

complicated: hard to understand

discrimination: unfairly treating people unequally because of their race or beliefs

equality: the state of being equal

exposition: a public show

industrial: relating to factories where products are made

inequality: the state of being unequal

influence: to have an effect on

legacy: something that is passed down from someone

legislature: a lawmaking body

reality: the real and true situation

FOR MORE INFORMATION

BOOKS

Buckley, James, Jr. *Who Was Booker T. Washington?* New York, NY: Penguin Workshop, 2018.

Harris, Duchess. *Booker T. Washington: Leader and Educator.* Minneapolis, MN: Abdo Publishing, 2020.

Jones-Radgowski, Jehan. *Booker T. Washington.* North Mankato, MN: Capstone Press, 2020.

WEBSITES

Booker T. Washington
www.encyclopediaofalabama.org/article/h-1506
Find a lengthy account of Booker's life on this site, along with some rare photos.

Booker T. Washington, Educator and Inspirational Source
aaregistry.org/storybooker-t-washington-educator-and-inspirational-source
Discover more facts about Booker's life here.

Dr. Booker Taliaferro Washington
www.tuskegee.edu/discover-tu/tu-presidents/booker-t-washington
Learn more about Booker T. Washington on this website.

Publisher's note to educators and parents: Our editors have carefully reviewed these websites to ensure that they are suitable for students. Many websites change frequently, however, and we cannot guarantee that a site's future contents will continue to meet our high standards of quality and educational value. Be advised that students should be closely supervised whenever they access the Internet.

INDEX